AIR POLLUTION

Gary Lopez

Designed by Rita Marshall
with the help of Thomas Lawton

© *1992 Creative Education, Inc.*
123 South Broad Street,
Mankato, Minnesota 56001

Photography by
Todd Anderson, Frank Balthis,
Gary Braasch, Explorer,
Tommy Iorio, Llewellyn,
Ancil Nance, Minden Pictures,
Richard Small, Starlight,
Weatherstock, and
Jerome Wyckoff

Library of Congress
Cataloging-in-Publication Data

Lopez, Gary.
Air pollution / by Gary Lopez.
p. cm.
Summary: Discusses the causes of air
pollution all over the world, the
"domino effect" that can occur when
people make wholesale changes to the
environment, and the urgency of
stopping the poisoning of our air.
ISBN 0-88682-427-3
1. Air—Pollution—Juvenile
literature.
[1. Air—Pollution. 2. Pollution.]
I. Title.   91-485
TD883.13.L66   1991   CIP
363.73' 92—dc20   AC

In Memory of

GEORGE R. PETERSON, SR.

6

More than two billion years ago, the worst ecological disaster in Earth's history began to unfold. The simple bacteria that thrived in the ancient oceans dumped huge amounts of toxic waste into their environment. The waste accumulated to higher and higher levels, until eventually it killed the bacteria themselves, as well as much of the other life inhabiting the Earth. The deadly waste was oxygen.

The ocean.

Of course, oxygen is not a deadly poison to us, or to most organisms now living on the planet. But things were much different on Earth two billion years ago. Then, there was little oxygen in the atmosphere and to most living things oxygen was a poison.

The global contamination of the atmosphere with oxygen was an important event for the surviving residents of Earth for two reasons. First, the oxygen-rich air allowed new forms of life to flourish. Second, it demonstrated that living things could have a catastrophic impact on the chemistry of the planet; they could even entirely remake the atmosphere.

Earth and the moon seen from space.

For the next two billion years, the concentrations of different gases in the earth's atmosphere rose and fell with volcanic eruptions, ice ages, and other natural events. Then, in the mid 1800s, a new type of atmospheric change began. The change was caused by a single species whose population numbers had grown dramatically. The species was *Homo Sapiens*—humans—and the change was *Air Pollution* caused by human factories.

The spread of factories across Western Europe and North America was known as the *Industrial Revolution*. One result of industrialization was a revolutionary improvement in the standard of living for many people, but another result was a revolutionary increase in the amounts of coal, oil, and other *Fossil Fuels* that were burned. Factories needed a great deal of energy, and fossil fuels were the way to fill that need.

Steam pours out of a volcano.

In the beginning, the air pollution that came with burning coal was considered to be a small price to pay for the wealth that came from industry. In fact, a thick cloud of grey coal smoke hanging over a city was looked upon as a sign of prosperity and power. More and more factories were built, surrounded by an ever-expanding sea of worker residences and shops. By the mid 1900s, the industrial world was dedicated to a course that required vast amounts of energy. There was no turning back.

Landscape of industry.

15

Today, fossil fuel use has grown to a level thousands of times higher than that of the early days of the industrial revolution. The air pollution from factories is now mixed with pollution from electricity-generating power plants and automobiles. Because of the automobile, every urban area in the world suffers from some level of air pollution. In Los Angeles, the air is unfit to breathe one day out of two, according to government standards. In Mexico City, children faint during school recess because of the choking smog.

Pollution north of Los Angeles.
Inset: Power plant stacks.

The problem of pollution has grown from being a concern of cities to being a threat to rural areas downwind. Clouds of airborne pollutants are blown from urban areas to the outlying countryside. Because of the pollution, dozens of national parks in the United States frequently violate federal clean air regulations. Forests, lakes, and wildlife in the United States, Canada, and Europe have been destroyed by a dangerous form of this traveling air pollution called *Acid Rain*.

Smokestacks pump out airborne pollution.

Acid rain is caused by sulfur and nitrogen chemicals in coal smoke and auto exhaust. These chemicals mix with the water in clouds to form powerful acids. Many coal-burning power plants have tall smokestacks up to four hundred feet high. The purpose of these enormous stacks is to keep coal smoke high above ground level so that it is not a nuisance to people living nearby. Unfortunately, the tall stacks inject coal smoke *so* high into the atmosphere that the resulting acid clouds can be carried by the wind to areas thousands of miles away.

In the midwestern United States, there is a concentration of coal-burning factories and power plants, as well as plenty of cars. Since the prevailing winds blow to the northeast, the acid clouds formed in the Midwest are carried to New York, Vermont, New Hampshire, and even into Canada. The pollution in these clouds falls to the ground as acid rain and snow. The acid weakens the pine, fir, and spruce trees in the forests, and kills fish and other animals in the lakes and streams. Across New England and Canada, more than seventeen thousand lakes have been damaged by acid rain.

Pollution over Arizona.

In Europe, the effects of acid rain were first noticed in the 1960s. In Germany, Czechoslovakia, and Poland, whole forests were destroyed. There was also extensive damage to many stone buildings and monuments. A mineral called *Limestone* is dissolved by acid. Buildings containing limestone were slowly melted by seasons of acid rain. Masons and stonecutters now work year-round to replace acid-damaged stones in ancient cathedrals and churches. Some of these holy shrines, which have survived seven hundred years of wars and weather, are now in danger of being destroyed by a few decades of polluted air.

Pages 20-21: Trees suffer from acid rain.
Page 21: The destructive effects of acid rain.

Understanding and preventing acid rain has become a worldwide focus of scientific research. One group of scientists, in the Adirondack Mountains of New York state, studies the acid clouds themselves. The research is done at a mountaintop station that is regularly covered by passing storm clouds. To collect cloud water, scientists venture outside the lab into the heart of active storm clouds where temperatures dip far below freezing and winds gust to fifty miles per hour. This research has revealed that clouds are like great mops, sweeping pollutants from the air. A cloud traveling from the Midwest is often laden with toxic chemicals and has an acid content similar to that of vinegar.

Clouds may release acid as well as rain.

Burning fossil fuels causes other air pollution problems besides acid rain. Another important concern is the release of a gas called *Carbon Dioxide,* or CO_2. In small amounts, CO_2 is not poisonous to people or other living things. In fact, nearly all animals make and release CO_2 every day. Carbon dioxide only becomes a problem when it builds up in the atmosphere and changes the way the sun warms the Earth. This warming problem is called the *Greenhouse Effect.* It works this way: Heat from the sun strikes the Earth. Some of the heat is absorbed by the Earth, but much of it is released back into space. Extra CO_2 in the atmosphere acts like the glass of a greenhouse and traps heat, causing the Earth to get hotter and hotter.

Although the temperature increase due to the greenhouse effect may only be a few degrees, it still might cause drastic changes around the world. An increase of a few degrees could cause shifts in climate and rainfall patterns, turning fertile land into deserts. It could also partially melt the polar ice caps, causing a rise in sea level which would lead to the flooding of coastal cities, such as Miami and Tokyo.

Industrial pollution contributes to the greenhouse effect.

People have burned so much fossil fuel since the beginning of the industrial revolution, it is estimated that the amount of CO_2 in the Earth's atmosphere has increased by nearly 25 percent. Today, factories and autos are not the only important CO_2 contributors. Each year, nearly forty million acres of tropical rain forest are burned and cleared, releasing 1.7 billion tons of CO_2 into the atmosphere. The forest is usually burned by farmers and ranchers who are making way for crops and cattle. One of the great tragedies of this "slash and burn" farming technique is that forests, which require decades to regrow, are destroyed to open up land where the soil is so thin and fragile that it will support crops for only two or three seasons. The farmer is then forced to move on, abandoning the useless land, and slash and burn again.

Slash and burn farming in Mexico.

In addition to carbon dioxide, forest burning indirectly produces another gas called *Methane* which also contributes to the greenhouse effect. Methane is a naturally occurring gas produced by bacteria that live in rice paddies and landfills, and inside cattle and termites. When a forest is clear, not all of the wood is completely burned. Termites move in and eat the surviving wood. A product of their digestion is methane. Since termites are tiny insects, it might be hard to imagine how the quantity of methane they produce could contribute to the greenhouse effect. But termites do have an impact because of their sheer numbers. There is an estimated three-quarters of a ton of termites for every person on Earth, and the number of termites is growing as more rain forest is burned. In addition, methane is hundreds of times more effective than CO_2 at producing the greenhouse effect.

Termites feeding on wood.
Inset: The charred remains of a fire.

Two important ideas are demonstrated by this description of slash and burn agriculture. The first idea is the *Connectedness of Nature.* It is almost comical to think that termites eating charred wood in the rain forests might cause Miami to be submerged by the rising sea; however, this is an example of the unexpected "domino effect" that can occur when people make wholesale changes to the environment. Not just the living things, but also the land, water, and air of the Earth are strongly interdependent. A change in one will result in a "push and shove" rearrangement of all.

Smog over the industrial Northeast.

The second idea revealed by the description of slash and burn agriculture is that air pollution has become a global problem and to solve it will require *Global Cooperation*. It would be simple to demand that peasant farmers stop slash and burn practices, but to do so would be to demand that they stop providing for their families. It was not too long ago that the United States and other western countries were clearing vast tracts of land as well. When the pilgrims landed at Plymouth Rock, the forest of the eastern seaboard region was so dense it was nearly impenetrable. Four hundred years later, it is nearly all gone, a victim of our progress. The South American and Asian countries now burning the rain forests are much like we were a few hundred years ago. How can we be critical?

Forest fire in Oregon.

34

In any case, the CO_2 and methane that result from slash and burn farming are only a fraction of what is released by industry and autos every year. The greatest responsibility for improving the quality of the air lies with the industrial countries of North America and Europe. The key is *Conservation*. If we can burn less fossil fuel and use what we do burn more efficiently, air pollution might no longer be a problem. If we could burn cleaner, low-sulfur coal and install sulfur-removal devices in power plant smoke-stacks, acid rain might begin to disappear.

Rush-hour traffic.

Listing the solutions to the problem of air pollution is easy, but changing peoples' habits is difficult. Things that were once luxuries and conveniences have become necessities for many of us—for example, air conditioning. The fossil fuels burned to cool our homes and offices each summer constitute a major portion of the energy we use annually. In addition, nearly all of us ride in cars that have air conditioning; the chemicals used in auto air conditioners may be one of the greatest hazards to the quality of the world's air.

Day and night, cars are a major source of air pollution.

The chemicals are called *Chlorofluorocarbons,* or CFCs for short. They are used not only for air conditioning, but also for cleaning computer parts, as aerosol propellants, and in the manufacture of styrofoam fast-food containers. In many ways, CFCs are chemicals that symbolize our prosperity. CFCs also represent a serious threat to the environment for two reasons. First, they add to the greenhouse effect. In fact, they are thousands of times more effective at trapping heat than CO_2. Second, CFCs destroy an important gas in the upper atmosphere called *Ozone.* Ozone is a rare form of oxygen that helps block harmful rays from the sun called ultraviolet, or UV, rays. Without ozone to stop them, *UV Rays* would bombard the Earth, causing disease and death to nearly all living things.

Pittsburgh early in the day.

Scientists have documented a decrease in average ozone levels worldwide, but the worst ozone decline has occurred over the continent of Antarctica. Each summer, the ozone protecting Antarctica nearly disappears, allowing the UV rays of the sun to pour through. Most scientists think that this hole in the ozone is caused by CFCs. How the ozone hole will affect the wildlife in Antarctica is still unclear. What is becoming clear, however, is that CFCs are destroying the ozone in the upper atmosphere, and may be endangering the planet.

A smokestack blocks the sun.

40

Air Pollution here on Earth is largely a side effect of human prosperity. With each new gadget that devours energy, we pour more waste into the atmosphere. We must realize soon that by poisoning the air, we are poisoning ourselves. If we don't, Homo sapiens may suffer the same fate as those simple bacteria that dominated the Earth more than two billion years ago.

Los Angeles smog.